From the Bible-Teaching Ministry of

CHARLES R. SWINDOLL

Living WATER *FOR A* THIRSTY *World*

D1026069

LifeMaps

Insight for Living

LIVING WATER for a THIRSTY WORLD
A LIFEMAPS BOOK

From the Bible-Teaching Ministry of Charles R. Swindoll

Charles R. Swindoll has devoted his life to the clear, practical teaching and application of God's Word and His grace. Chuck currently is the senior pastor of Stonebriar Community Church in Frisco, Texas; but his listening audience extends far beyond this local church body. As a leading program in Christian broadcasting, *Insight for Living* airs in major Christian radio markets around the world, reaching people groups in languages they can understand. Chuck's extensive writing ministry has also served the body of Christ worldwide and his leadership as president and now chancellor of Dallas Theologicala Seminary has helped prepare and equip a new generation for ministry.

Copyright © 2007 by Charles R. Swindoll, Inc.

Chapter One was adapted from the original sermon titled "Mr. Smith, Meet Your Substitute," Copyright ℗ © 1985 by Charles R. Swindoll, Inc. from the series *Growing Deep in the Christian Life*, Copyright ℗ © 1985, 1991 by Charles R. Swindoll, Inc.

Chapter Two was adapted from the original sermon "Strengthening Your Grip on Evangelism," Copyright ℗ © 1981 by Charles R. Swindoll, Inc. from the series *Strengthening your Grip*, Copyright ℗ © 1980, 1981 by Charles R. Swindoll, Inc.

Chapter Three, "Tools for Evangelism," was adapted from *Passion for the Gospel*, Copyright © 2006 by Charles R. Swindoll, Inc. and Greg Laurie.

Published by
IFL Publishing House
A Division of Insight for Living
Post Office Box 251007
Plano, Texas 75025-1007

Based upon the original outlines, charts, and transcripts of Charles R. Swindoll's sermons, *Living Water for a Thirsty World* was collaboratively developed by the Creative Ministries Department of Insight for Living.

Editor in Chief: Cynthia Swindoll, President, Insight for Living
Executive Vice President: Wayne Stiles, Th.M., D.Min., Dallas Theological Seminary
Director of Creative Ministries: Michael J. Svigel, Th.M., Ph.D. candidate,
    Dallas Theological Seminary
Editor: Cari Harris, B.A. Journalism, Grand Canyon University
Copy Editors: Jim Craft, M.A., English, Mississippi College
    Melanie Munnell, M.A. Humanities, The University of Texas at Dallas
Project Coordinator, Communications: Dusty R. Crosby, B.S., Communications,
    Dallas Baptist University
Proofreader: Joni Halpin, B.S., Accountancy, Miami University
Cover Designer: Steven Tomlin, Embry-Riddle Aeronautical University, 1992-1995
Production Artists: Sharon D. Chandler, B.A., German, Texas Tech University
    Nancy Gustine, B.F.A., Advertising Art, University of North Texas
Cover Photo: Copyright © 2007 iStock Images, Slawomir Jastrzebski

ISBN: 978-1-57972-764-2
Printed in the United States of America

Table of Contents

A Letter from Chuck

When I was growing up, I never knew cursing, drinking, divorce, or what people commonly call "the wild life." And believe it or not, at the time I didn't know the rest of the world was any different from my secure and well-protected world. Today many feel that growing up in such a sheltered environment, free from the dangers of the world, has nothing but advantages . . . but there's also a downside. That type of isolation can lull us to sleep and rob us of our passion for the gospel.

How so?

Until you step out the door of your comfortable Christian surroundings into the raw depravity of the world, you can't fully understand humanity's *desperate* need for the life-changing gospel. I know the temptation to stay inside our Christian cloisters is great. That's why some of us need to be shocked out of our "Christian club" mentalities. It took a stint in the Marine Corps for me to become fully aware of the depths of sinful depravity . . . and to catch a passion for the gospel's transforming power.

Before putting my seabag down on the floor of that Quonset hut in Okinawa, I distinctly remember thinking: *Before I even put these clothes in this little footlocker, I've got to decide whether or not I'm going to walk with Christ.*

Was I going to be His witness here, at the "remotest part of the earth" (Acts 1:8), or ignore my roots, compromise my convictions, and just blend in? If I stayed quiet nobody would've known.

Silence always seems like the easiest way, doesn't it? Have you ever squirmed in your seat on an airplane, wondering if you should bring up spiritual things with the passenger beside you? Do you know the feeling of standing on a new neighbor's doorstep—palms sweating, heart pounding—struggling with whether simply to welcome that person to the neighborhood or to take the opportunity to invite him or her to church?

It takes courage to step out from the safety of the hothouse of Christianity and walk through the open door of evangelism. It is risky. Not even making friends is easy. A few snide comments from critics, an insulting remark from an atheist, or bad press from a journalist can quickly deflate our passion for evangelism. We can lose heart by focusing so much on the staggering task before us that we decide to sit still and keep quiet rather than make waves and "rock the boat."

Timidity . . . fear . . . indecision—this trio of thieves will rob your commitment to the gospel, leaving you numb to the needs of the world. Resist them. Ignore the overwhelming odds. Forget about the "what-ifs" of rejection and derision. Frankly, both are rare. Instead, think about what might happen if you *don't* share the gospel. Even though you can't do everything, you *can* do something.

I often return to that critical moment so many years ago on Okinawa. It challenged my views about people, about evangelism, and about my need to step through the doors of opportunity God placed before me. Because I decided to take that step into the fallen world as Christ's ambassador, I had the privilege of leading seven (perhaps eight) of the Marines in our hut to Christ. That may not sound like a "great awakening" to you, but believe me—seven or eight souls out of forty-eight Marines was a *revival*! And though I've always been grateful for the moral foundation I had as a child, only when I took that first, risky step into the world of sinners did my heart for evangelism spark into a fire that has never flamed out.

This book is designed to help you take those same steps with boldness rather than fear, with confidence rather than hesitation. You may only be one person, but you can still make a difference. *So, please, make a difference!* God has opened a door for you to share the gospel with those around you. Will you make a decision to step through that door? How about starting *today*!

Charles R. Swindoll

At its heart, a map is the distillation of the experience of travelers—those who have journeyed in the past and recorded their memories in the form of pictures and symbols. The map represents the cumulative wisdom of generations of travelers, put together for the benefit of those now wishing to make that same journey.

To undertake a journey with a map is therefore to rely on the wisdom of the past. It is to benefit from the hard-won knowledge of those who have explored the unknown and braved danger in order to serve those who will follow in their footsteps. Behind the lines and symbols of the map lie countless personal stories—stories the map itself can never tell. Yet sometimes those stories need to be told, just as the hard-won insights of coping with traveling can encourage, inspire, and assist us.[1]

—Alister E. McGrath

Welcome to *LifeMaps*

On a journey, the important thing is not speed as much as it is *direction*.

But sometimes heading the right way requires some guidance. Think about it. You would never set out on a long road-trip without first making sure you knew which direction to go, right? You'd consult a map. For many people, the journey toward a deeper and more meaningful relationship with God lies along new or unfamiliar ground. They need directions; they need a map. And, even with a map, sometimes you can still get lost. When you do, it's the locals who know best—those who have been down the same roads. That's why this book is designed to be completed in concert with someone else. Wise friends or counselors can encourage us in our spiritual growth and help us avoid pitfalls along our paths.

Using *LifeMaps*

LifeMaps provides opportunities for individuals to interact with the Bible in different settings and on several levels, depending upon your particular needs or interests. *LifeMaps* also places a tool in the hands of pastors and other Christian leaders, helping them guide others along a journey of spiritual growth through the study and application of the Bible.

For Individuals

You can use *LifeMaps* in your personal devotions to gain God's perspective on a particular area of Christian living. In addition to offering engaging chapters to read, *LifeMaps* can further your journey of spiritual growth with the help of penetrating questions and opportunities for personal application.

LifeMaps can also serve as a first step to healing or resolving an issue that continues to plague you. Read, reflect, answer the questions, and then contact a competent, mature, godly man or woman to discuss the topic as it relates to your personal situation. This individual can be a pastor, a counselor, or even one of our staff here at Insight for Living in the Pastoral Ministries department (see page 79 for information on how to contact Insight for Living). This step is an essential part of the journey.

For Pastors and Counselors

LifeMaps is designed to guide individuals through an engaging, in-depth study of the Word of God, freeing you to help them apply the truths in even more specific and personal ways. As a vital first step in the counseling process, each volume lays a solid biblical, theological, and practical foundation upon which you can build. Encouraging individuals to work through the book on their own allows them the time necessary for personal reflection and education while enabling you to target your ministry of personal interaction and discipleship to their particular needs.

For Groups

LifeMaps can serve as a curriculum for home Bible studies, Sunday school classes, and accountability or discipleship groups. Each book in the series contains enough material for group discussion of key questions and noteworthy passages. *LifeMaps* can also foster meaningful interaction for pastors, elders, staff, and Christian leaders during staff devotionals, leadership retreats, or board meetings.

Suggestions for Study

Whether you use *LifeMaps* in a group, in a counseling setting, in the classroom, or for personal study, we trust it will prove to be an invaluable guide as you seek deeper intimacy with God and growth in godliness. In any setting, the following suggestions will make *LifeMaps* more beneficial for you.

- Begin each chapter with prayer, asking God to teach you through His Word and to open your heart to the self-discovery afforded by the questions and text.

- Read the chapters with pen in hand. Underline any thoughts, quotes, or verses that stand out to you. Use the pages provided at the end of each section to record any questions you may have, especially if you plan to meet with others for discussion.

- Have your Bible handy. Following chapters one and two, you'll be prompted to read relevant sections of Scripture and answer questions related to the topic.

- As you complete each chapter, close with prayer, asking God to apply the wisdom and principles to your life by His Holy Spirit. Then watch God work! He may bring people and things into your life that will challenge your attitudes and actions. You may gain new insight about the world and your faith. You may find yourself applying this new wisdom in ways you never expected.

May God's Word illumine your path as you begin your journey. We trust that this volume in the *LifeMaps* series will be a trustworthy guide to learning and to your spiritual growth.

Living
WATER
FOR A
THIRSTY
World

Chapter I

"Mr. Smith, Meet Your Substitute"

When Peter Marshall preached, people listened. Even if they didn't believe what he said. Even when they said they were not interested. The man refused to be ignored.

Who can fully explain it? There was something about his winsome, contagious style that made it impossible for people not to listen. Even when he became chaplain of the United States Senate and prayed more than he preached, his prayers became legendary. Ask those who were fortunate enough to have heard him. They'll tell you that everywhere Marshall preached, crowds gathered. Even if it was raining or snowing outside, the main floor and balconies would be full, packed with people, and many others who could not find a seat were willing to stand and listen as he spoke the truth of the living God.

Peter Marshall was Scottish, but his popularity went deeper than his Scottish brogue. And it certainly was more than just a charming personality or his well-timed humor that would win a hearing. The man had a way with men as well as women. He was admired by both. A man's man and yet a sensitive touch. At times one would swear he was more a poet than a preacher. He wasn't extemporaneous. To the surprise of many,

Marshall *read* his sermons, considered a no-no by most professors of homiletics. But I suppose if one could read like Peter Marshall, who really cared if he broke that rule?

A contemporary of Marshall's said it best with this terse analysis:

> What Peter Marshall says, you never forget. . . . But it isn't *how* he says it, so much as it is *what* he says, you never forget. . . . He has a gift for word pictures, for little dramas and folksy incidents; he takes you out on the road to Galilee and makes you think you belong there, and he brings you back sharply to Main Street. He never preaches over your head. [2]

Perhaps that, more than any other single ingredient, was the secret of the man's success. He certainly had the ability to go much deeper, but he purposely restrained himself. He was always cognizant of his audience. Because he was from an impoverished background, he understood the common man and woman. So he spoke in plain terms, colorful to be sure, and dramatic at times; but people never had trouble connecting with what Peter Marshall was saying.

Listen to a part of one of his sermons:

> Our country is full of Joneses, and they all have problems of one kind or another. "All God's chillun' got trouble these days."
>
> The Church has always contended that God can solve these problems through the individual's personal fellowship with a living Lord.

Let's put the question bluntly, as
bluntly as Mr. Jones would put it.

Can you and I really have communion with Christ as we would with
earthly friends?

Can we know personally the same
Jesus whose words are recorded in the
New Testament, Who walked the dusty
trails of Galilee two thousand years ago?

I don't mean can we treasure His
words or try to follow His example or
imagine Him.

I mean, is He really alive? Can we
actually meet Him, commune with Him,
ask His help for our everyday affairs?

The Gospel writers say "yes." A
host of men and women down the ages
say "yes." And the church says "yes." [3]

Appropriately, he entitled that sermon "Mr. Jones,
Meet the Master." I have hitchhiked on the man's idea
by choosing a similar title for this chapter: "Mr. Smith,
Meet Your Substitute." I figure that Mr. Jones has been
picked on long enough. We need to give Jones a break.
So, Mr. Smith, this is for you . . . as well as for your
wife . . . and the Johnsons, the Franklins, the Clarks,
the Parkers, or whatever your name may be. Because
I'm writing to the common man or woman today who
happens to find himself or herself in the same precari-
ous predicament.

The predicament is called sin. And that's why you
need a substitute.

Four Major Issues

Let's talk about that "why" issue.

The sixth book in the New Testament is the book of Romans. In the third chapter of that book (which is actually a letter originally written to some people who lived in Rome, Italy, in the first century), you may be surprised to hear that your biography is included. It doesn't actually include your name or your place of residence, but it does tell the story of your personal life. The stuff it mentions isn't very attractive, I should warn you, but it is the truth. And so, Mr. Smith, this is your life. I mentioned it early, but it bears repeating.

Our Condition: Totally Depraved

> What then? Are we better than they?
> Not at all; for we have already charged
> that both Jews and Greeks are all under
> sin; as it is written,

> "There is none righteous, not even one;
> There is none who understands,
> There is none who seeks for God;
> All have turned aside, together they
>   have become useless;
> There is none who does good,
> There is not even one."
> "Their throat is an open grave,
> With their tongues they keep
>   deceiving,"
> "The poison of asps is under their lips";
> "Whose mouth is full of cursing and
>   bitterness";

"Their feet are swift to shed blood,
Destruction and misery are in
    their paths,
And the path of peace they have not
    known."
"There is no fear of God before their
    eyes."

Now we know that whatever the
Law says, it speaks to those who are
under the Law, so that every mouth
may be closed and all the world may
become accountable to God; because
by the works of the Law no flesh will
be justified in His sight; for through the
Law comes the knowledge of sin. . . .
For all have sinned and fall short of the
glory of God. (Romans 3:9–20, 23)

Honestly, now, does that sound like your life? Is
that a fairly apt description of the inner you . . . down
where nobody else can look? I think so. How do I know?
Because it describes me, too. Even when we try to hide
it, even when we put on our sophisticated best, it comes
out when we least expect it.

Maybe you heard about the large commercial jet
that was flying from Chicago to Los Angeles. About half
an hour after takeoff, the passengers on board heard a
voice over the loud speaker. "Good morning, ladies and
gentlemen. This is a recording. You have the privilege
of being on the first wholly electronically controlled jet.
This plane has no pilot or copilot and no flight engineer
because they are no longer needed. But do not worry,
nothing can possibly go wrong, go wrong, go wrong, go
wrong, go wrong, go wrong. . . ."

God's Character: Infinitely Holy

Next, my friend Smith, I should mention something that will only add insult to injury. God is righteous, perfect, and infinitely holy. That's His standard. It is sometimes called "glory" in the New Testament. We looked earlier at Romans 3:23. Let me paraphrase it:

> For all have sinned [that's our condition] and fall short of the perfection, holiness, righteousness, and glory [that's His standard] of God.

Unlike all humanity, God operates from a different level of expectation. His existence is in the realm of absolute perfection. He requires the same from others. Whoever hopes to relate to Him must be as righteous as He is righteous. How different from us! To relate to me you don't have to be perfect. In fact, if you act like you are, I get very uncomfortable. "Just be what you are," we say. But God is not like that. God doesn't shrug, wink, and say, "Ah, that's okay."

Let me put it another way. God's triangle is perfect. And in order for us to fellowship with Him, our triangles must be congruent. The sides and the angles must match. So must the space within. Perfection requires matching perfection.

Ah, there's the rub! We have sinned and fallen short of the perfection of God. No one qualifies as perfect. Don't misunderstand; there are times that our goodness is astounding. We take great strides, we produce great achievements. We may even surprise ourselves with periodic times of goodness, gentleness, and compassion. But "perfect"? Never. Or "infinitely holy"? How about "pure"? No, only God is those things. Romans 3:21 calls God's perfection, holiness, and purity "the righteousness of God [that] has been manifested, being witnessed by the Law and the Prophets." Compared to *that* standard, all humans come up short.

The New Living Translation puts it like this:

> For no one can ever be made right with
> God by doing what the law commands.
> The law simply shows us how sinful we
> are. (Romans 3:20)

Isn't that the truth? He is perfect and spotless white. Not a taint of gray. Not a hint of blue. And along comes our blue rectangle, trying to work its way into that perfect, holy, and pure triangle. And the two just won't match! There is no way, Mr. Smith, that we can match His righteousness.

Our Need: A Substitute

Here we are, sinners by birth, sinners by nature, sinners by choice, trying to reach and attain a relationship with the holy God who made us. And we fall short. We can't make it because we're spiritually crippled. In fact, the New Testament teaches that we're "dead in trespasses and sin."

What do we need? Let me put it plain and simple, Mr. Smith; we need help outside ourselves.

We need some way to become clean within so that we can relate to a God who is perfect. Scripture says, "God is Light, and in Him there is no darkness at all" (1 John 1:5). If we hope to know God, walk with God, and relate to God, we must be able to stand the scrutiny of that kind of light. But our light is out. We're all dark, and He is all light. In his immortal hymn, Charles Wesley envisioned us in a dark dungeon, chained and helpless—

> Long my imprisoned spirit lay
> Fast bound in sin and nature's night. [4]

We can't get out of the dungeon, not even if we try. Our own sin holds us in bondage. We need someone to rescue us from the hole. We need an advocate in the courtroom of justice. We need someone who will present our case. We need someone to be our substitute. So God provided the Savior.

God's Provision: A Savior

> [We] are justified freely by his grace through the redemption that came by Christ Jesus. God presented him as a sacrifice of atonement, through faith in his blood. He did this to demonstrate his justice, because in his forbearance he had left the sins committed beforehand unpunished—he did it to demonstrate his justice at the present time, so as to be just and the one who justifies those who have faith in Jesus. (Romans 3:24–26 NIV)

Is that great news? Mr. Smith, you have just been introduced to your Substitute. He is Christ, the sinless and perfect Son of God. He is the One who accomplished your rescue. It occurred on a cross. It was effective because He was the only One who could qualify as our substitute before God. Sin requires a penalty—death—in order for God's righteous demands to be satisfied. The ransom must be paid. And Christ fills that role to perfection. You and I need to be washed. We need to be made sparkling clean. And God can't give up on His plan, for He hates sin. Being perfect, He cannot relate to sinful things. He couldn't even if He tried, because His nature is repelled by sin. Sin calls for judgment. And that is why the cross is so significant. It became the place of judgment. It was there the price was paid in full.

In verse 24 of Romans 3, the term *justified* appears. Let's work with that word a few moments. It does not simply mean "just as if I'd never sinned." That doesn't go far enough! Neither does it mean that God makes me righteous so that I never sin again. It means "to be declared righteous." Justification is God's merciful act whereby He declares righteous the believing sinner while he is still in a sinning state. He sees us in our need, wallowing around in the swamp of our sin. He sees us looking to Jesus Christ and trusting Him completely by faith to cleanse us from our sin. And though we come to Him with all of our needs and in all of our darkness, God says to us, "Declared righteous! Forgiven! Pardoned!" Wesley caught the significance of all this as he completed that same stanza:

> Thine eye diffused a quick'ning ray,
> I woke, the dungeon flamed with light;
> My chains fell off, my heart was free;
> I rose, went forth and followed Thee.[5]

I like the way Billy Graham imagines all this:

> Picture a courtroom. God the Judge is seated in the judge's seat, robed in splendor. You are arraigned before Him. He looks at you in terms of His own righteous nature as it is expressed in the moral law. He speaks to you:

> GOD: John (or) Mary, have you loved Me with all your heart?

> JOHN/MARY: No, Your Honor.

> GOD: Have you loved others as you have loved yourself?

> JOHN/MARY: No, Your Honor.

GOD: Do you believe you are a
sinner and that Jesus died for
your sins?

JOHN/MARY: Yes, Your Honor.

GOD: Then your penalty has been
paid by Jesus Christ on the
cross and you are pardoned. . . .
Because Christ is righteous and
you believe in Christ, I now
declare you legally righteous.

Can you imagine what a newspaper-
man would do with this event?

SINNER PARDONED — GOES
TO LIVE WITH JUDGE

It was a tense scene when John
and Mary stood before the Judge. [He]
transferred all of the guilt to Jesus Christ,
who died on a cross for John and Mary.

After John and Mary were pardoned, the Judge invited them to come
to live with Him forever.

The reporter on such a story like
that would never be able to understand
the irony of such a scene, unless he had
been introduced to the Judge before-
hand and knew His character.

Pardon and Christ's righteousness
come to us only when we totally trust
ourselves to Jesus as our Lord and
Savior. When we do this, God welcomes
us into His intimate favor. Clothed in
Christ's righteousness we can now enjoy
God's fellowship. [6]

All of that is included in what it means to be justified. I come to Him in all my need. I am hopelessly lost, spiritually dead. And I present myself to Christ just as I am. I have nothing to give that would earn my way in. If I could I would, but I can't. So the only way I can present myself to Him in my lost condition is by faith. Coming in my need, expressing faith in His Son who died for me, I understand that God sees me coming by faith and admitting my sinfulness. At that epochal moment, He declares me righteous.

On occasion I think of the cross as a sponge . . . a "spiritual sponge" that has taken the sins of mankind—past, present, and future—and absorbed them all. At one awful moment, Christ bore our sins, thus satisfying the righteous demands of the Father, completely and instantaneously clearing up my debt. My sin is forgiven. My enslavement is broken. I am set free from sin's power once and for all. *Redemption*, another significant word in verse 24, also occurs. I am set at liberty so as never to come back to the slave market of sin—never again in bondage to it. And remember, the rescue occurred because of what *Christ* did—not because of what I did.

I love the way Romans 3:28 reads:

> For we maintain that a man is justified
> by faith apart from works of the Law.

I remember hearing a seasoned Bible teacher say, "Man is incurably addicted to doing something for his own salvation." What a waste! Scripture teaches that salvation is a by-faith, not by-works, transaction.

In Romans 4:4–5, this is made ever so clear:

> Now to the one who works, his wage
> is not credited as a favor, but as what
> is due. But to the one who does not

work, but believes in Him who justifies
the ungodly, his faith is credited as
righteousness.

Just think of your paycheck, Mr. Smith. When your
boss or someone from your boss's office brings you your
paycheck, you take it. You take it, I might add, without a
great deal of gratitude. You don't drop to your knees and
say, "Oh, thank you — thank you so very much for this
gift." You probably grab the check and don't give much
thought to saying thanks. Why? Because you *earned*
it. You worked *hard* for it. Now, if your boss attaches
a bonus of a thousand bucks (and maybe even adds,
"Though you're dropping in your efficiency, I want you
to know I love you"), wouldn't that be great? That would
be a miracle! There's a great difference between a wage
and a gift.

God looks at us in all of our need and He sees
nothing worth commending. Not only are we dropping
in our spiritual efficiency, we have no light, no holiness.
We're moving in the opposite direction, despising Him,
living in a dungeon of sin, habitually carrying out the
lifestyle of our sinful nature. Realizing our need, we
accept His miraculous, eternal bonus — the gift of His
Son. And in grace, our dungeon "flamed with light." You
and I didn't even deserve the light, yet He gave it to us
as an unmerited gift. Look again at verse 5:

But to the one who does not work,
but believes in Him who justifies the
ungodly, his faith is credited as
righteousness.

I love that verse! Because there's no way you and
I can get any credit. We're bound in a dungeon, lost
in ourselves. We don't even know where to find the

light. Even when we try, we are like the line out of the country-western song; we "look for love in all the wrong places."

This reminds me of the story I read about a drunk down on all fours late one night under a streetlight. He was groping around on the ground, feeling the cement, peering intently at the little cracks. And a friend drives up and says, "Sam, what are you doing there?" Sam answers, "I lost my wallet." So the friend gets out of his car, walks over, gets down on his hands and knees with him, and they both start looking. Neither one can find it. Finally the friend says to the drunk buddy:

> "Are you sure you lost the wallet here?"
>
> "Of course not! I dropped it half a block over there."
>
> "Then why are we looking here?"
>
> "Because there's no *streetlight* over there."

Mr. Smith, I'm going to level with you. I know you fairly well, even though we've never met. You read these words about the *gift* of eternal life and you simply cannot fathom them, so you won't take them. I mean, you've got your pride, so you will reject them. I can even imagine your reluctance: "Too good to be true, Chuck. Sounds great. Looks good in a book. And it's definitely an intriguing idea. Who wouldn't want to tell people that? But if I get into heaven, I'll earn it on my own."

Well, let me give you just a little logic to wrestle with. If you plan to work your way in, how much work is enough work to guarantee that you have made it? And if it's something you work for, why does God say in His Book that it's for "the one who does *not* work, but believes . . ." Romans 4:5, emphasis added)?

Let me spell it out:

God's Character:	Infinitely Holy
Our Condition:	Totally Depraved
Our Need:	A Substitute
God's Provision:	A Savior

When God provided the Savior, He said to each one of us, "Here is my Gift to you." How often, when folks hear that, they shake their heads and mumble, "I can't believe it."

In 2 Corinthians 5:20, we find these words:

Therefore, we are ambassadors for Christ, as though God were making an appeal through us; we beg you on behalf of Christ, be reconciled to God.

That's the message of this chapter in a nutshell. I beg you . . . be reconciled to God. Watch that barrier crumble, the one between you and God, as you step across by faith. Look at the next verse.

He made Him who knew no sin to be sin on our behalf, so that we might become the righteousness of God in Him.

Now, let me identify the pronouns:

He [God, the Father] made Him [God, the Son] who knew no sin to be sin on our behalf [that happened at the cross], so that we [the sinner] might become the righteousness of God in Him [Christ].

Let's boil it down:

God:	The Righteous
Christ:	The Sacrifice
We:	The Sinner
Christ:	The Life

How? The cross.

But how can the sinner in the black hole of his need ever know God in the spotless white of all His righteousness? Verse 21 tells us. By coming to know "Him who knew no sin," the One who became "sin on our behalf." Put your pride in your pocket, Mr. Smith. You need a substitute. You need a defense attorney . . . an eternal advocate. And in Christ—and Christ alone—you've got one.

Three Crucial Questions

Seems to me there are three crucial questions we must answer. Each has a two-word answer.

Question	Answer
1. Is there any hope for lost sinners?	Yes, Christ.
2. Isn't there any work for a seeker to do?	No, believe.
3. Is there any way for the saved to lose the gift?	No, never!

Now let me spell that out.

First question: Is there any hope for lost sinners? Yes, Christ. Not Christ and the church. Not Christ and good works. Not Christ and sincerity. Not Christ and giving up your sins. Not Christ and trying really hard.

Not Christ and baptism, Christ and christening, Christ and morality, or Christ and a good family. No! Christ (period). Otherwise, it's works. He died for our sins and was placed in the grave as proof of His death. He rose from the dead bodily, miraculously, in proof of His life beyond. If you believe that He died and rose for you, you have eternal life. It's a gift.

Second question: Isn't there any work for a seeker to do? Don't I have to add to it? Answer: No (period). Believe!

One of my favorite illustrations of the importance of believing and not working is to consider a nice meal you and I enjoy together. You invite me over. I come to your home. We have planned this for quite some time, and you've worked hard in the kitchen. You have prepared my favorite meal. You are thrilled because you have a great recipe. And I'm happy because it's going to be a delightful evening with you. I knock on your front door. I'm starved. We sit down together at the table, and you serve this delicious meal. We dine and dialogue together. What a thoroughly enjoyable evening!

Then, as I get up to leave, I reach into my pocket and say, "Now, what do I owe you?" You're *shocked*! That's an insult. You knew what I needed, and out of love for me, you fixed it and served it. Why, a major part of being a good host is that you pick up the tab. For me to suggest that I'll pay for it is like a slap in the face. You don't even want me to help with the dishes. Love motivated your giving me this great meal. It is your gift to me. To ask to pay for it repels your love.

Do you realize that there are men and women all around the world who are reaching in their pockets this very day saying, "Okay, God . . . how much do I owe you?"

I have communicated this same message for years, but I will never forget the time I had a lady come to the platform after a meeting to see me. She had dissolved in tears. She said, "Here's my Bible. Would you sign your autograph in the back, just your autograph? And then," she added, "would you put underneath it in quotes 'Salvation is a *gift*'?"

"You see," she explained, "my background is religious, and all my life I've worked so hard. All my friends are from that same religious background, and they are still working so hard. Now—for the first time in my life, I realized that God is really offering me a gift. The thing I have noticed about all of us, all these years, is that not one of us has ever been secure. We've never known that salvation was ours *forever*—because we worked so hard for it. Our plan was to keep working so we could keep it in us."

She had been reaching into her purse all these years, trying to pay God for His gift. Was it free? No, not really. It cost Christ His life at the cross many centuries ago.

Third question: Is there any way to lose the gift? No, never! Now stop and think before you disagree. Stay with biblical logic, not human reasoning. If you work for it, then you can certainly lose it. And that would mean it's not a gift; it's what you've earned. We really confuse things when we try to turn a gift into a wage. Furthermore, just as no one can say how much work is enough to earn it, no one can say how little work is enough to lose it.

Salvation is simply a gift. It's simple, but it wasn't easy. It's free, but it wasn't cheap. It's yours, but it isn't automatic. You must receive it. When you do, it is yours forever.

Two Possible Responses

We're back to basics, Mr. Smith. When you return to the roots of salvation, you can either believe and accept this gift, or you can refuse and reject it. And you can go right on living, by the way. You won't suddenly get struck by lightning if you reject Christ. I've noticed that God doesn't immediately start doing bad things to people who refuse His Son. He doesn't make you look foolish. He won't suddenly cut your legs off at the knees. He doesn't scar your face or make you lose your job. He doesn't keep your car from starting because you reject the message. He doesn't kill your closest friend or cause your mate to leave you as a judgment because you didn't believe. That's not the way God operates.

He simply waits.

And that fakes people out. That makes some folks think that if He really meant it, then He'd zap them for refusing to take His gift. No. Not necessarily. Those who think like that don't understand God. He holds out His grace and He makes it available even if we choose to reject it.

One Final Reminder

But I must remind you of something: You don't have forever. With no intention of manipulating you, you need to remember that death is certain. I wish I had kept track of the funeral services I have conducted in the last ten years on behalf of those who died before the age of fifty. Without trying to sound dramatic, I think it would shock you to know how many die before they turn fifty. And I'm sure some of them thought, "I've got a long time to go."

Listen, sin is terminal. And Mr. Smith, you've got that disease. It leads to death. It may not even be a year before you are gone . . . and you will have thought you had plenty of time.

I'm sure Peter Marshall thought he had a long, long time. May I return to his life? He was appointed to the Senate chaplaincy in early January 1947 . . . a specimen of good health. Yet it was just a shade beyond two years later when this forty-seven-year-old man was seized with a heart attack and died. He was as eloquent and creative as ever right up to the last . . . but within a matter of hours, his voice was hushed forever. Only the printed page speaks for Marshall today.

A sermon of his that one can never forget is what he called "The Tap on the Shoulder."

> If you were walking down the street, and someone came up behind you and tapped you on the shoulder . . . what would you do? Naturally, you would turn around. Well, that is exactly what happens in the spiritual world. A man walks on through life—with the external call ringing in his ears, but with no response stirring in his heart, and then suddenly, without any warning, the Spirit taps him on the shoulder. The tap on the shoulder is the almighty power of God acting without help or hindrance . . . so as to produce a new creature, and to lead him into the particular work which God has for him. [7]

Maybe as you've read this chapter, you've felt God's tap on your shoulder. If so, respond. Stop reading. Close the book, bow your head, and tell the Lord you have felt

His tap—and you want to accept His gift of eternal life. Thank Him for giving you His Son, Jesus Christ.

If you have done that, Mr. Smith . . . you have just met your Substitute.

Starting Your Journey

Individuals often resist the idea that they need a Savior. Instead, they point out all the good things they have been "doing," feeling that it would "balance out on the scales" when they stood before God. How might you respond to that line of reasoning?

_____

_____

_____

_____

To what Scriptures might you direct such an individual?

_____

_____

_____

_____

What illustrations could you use to help him or her get a grasp on the central truth of this chapter?

_____

_____

_____

_____

To *share* your faith, you need to be *aware* of your faith. Become familiar with basic Christian doctrine and a simple gospel presentation that clearly illustrates how we cannot reach God through our own efforts. Some helpful resources include the following:

- *Essential Truths: A Pocket Guide for Growing Deep* (Insight for Living)

- *Religions of the World Passport* (Insight for Living)

- *Steps to Peace with God* (Billy Graham)

- *The Four Spiritual Laws* (Campus Crusade for Christ)

- *The Bridge to Life* (NavPress)

- *May I Ask You a Question?* (EvanTell)

With which of these tools are you familiar?

_____

_____

_____

_____

Find a tract with which you are comfortable and purchase several copies of it — keeping one handy in your wallet, pocket, or purse. You might meet a Mr. Smith or Miss Smith this week who needs the Substitute.

This chapter looked closely at Romans 3 and 4. Carve out some time this week to get a feel for this liberating portion of Scripture. Read Romans 3 – 5, preferably in two different translations of Scripture. Ask the Lord to give you fresh insight as you trace this all-important faith-root.

What insights about humans, God, Christ, salvation, and the gospel do you see in Romans 3–5?

_____

_____

_____

_____

My Questions and Thoughts

My Questions and Thoughts

Chapter 2

Strengthening Your Grip on Evangelism

> The evangelistic harvest is always
> urgent. The destiny of men and of
> nations is always being decided. Every
> generation is strategic. We are not
> responsible for the past generation, and
> we cannot bear the full responsibility
> for the next one; but we do have our
> generation. God will hold us responsible
> as to how well we fulfill our responsi-
> bilities to this age and take advantage of
> our opportunities. [8]

Those are the words of Billy Graham. And the man ought
to know. He has spoken publicly about Christ to more
people in our generation than anyone else. His evangelistic crusades have had an impact on more cities around
the world and invaded more homes (thanks to television)
than any other evangelistic outreach in the history of
time. We cannot think of the name *Billy Graham* without
attaching the word *evangelism* to it. He has a strong grip
on the subject, but the question is, do we?

Probably not.

Most of us want to. We *wish* we did. We are certainly aware of the need and, if the whole truth could
be told, some of us have even taken courses to help us

become better at witnessing, but we still stumble. Our grip on evangelism is weak—embarrassingly weak.

A fellow pastor was honest enough to admit this in an article he wrote for a Christian magazine. Because it illustrates so well the problem all of us wrestle with, I want to share it with you. The pastor, dressed in a comfortable pair of old blue jeans, boarded a plane to return home. He settled into the last unoccupied seat next to a well-dressed businessman with the *Wall Street Journal* tucked under his arm. The minister, a little embarrassed over his casual attire, decided he'd look straight ahead and, for sure, stay out of any in-depth conversation. But the plan didn't work. The man greeted him, so, to be polite, the pastor asked about the man's work. Here's what happened:

> "I'm in the figure salon business. We can change a woman's self-concept by changing her body. It's really a very profound, powerful thing."
>
> His pride spoke between the lines.
>
> "You look my age," I said. "Have you been at this long?"
>
> "I just graduated from the University of Michigan's School of Business Administration. They've given me so much responsibility already, and I feel very honored. In fact, I hope to eventually manage the western part of the operation."
>
> "So, you are a national organization?" I asked, becoming impressed despite myself.
>
> "Oh, yes. We are the fastest growing company of our kind in the nation. It's

really good to be a part of an organization like that, don't you think?"

I nodded approvingly and thought, "Impressive. Proud of his work and accomplishments. . . . Why can't Christians be proud like that? Why are we so often apologetic about our faith and our church?"

Looking askance at my clothing, he asked the inevitable question, "And what do you do?" . . .

"It's interesting that we have similar business interests," I said. "You are in the body-changing business; I'm in the personality-changing business. We apply 'basic theocratic principles to accomplish indigenous personality modification.'"

He was hooked, but I knew he would never admit it. (Pride is powerful.)

"You know, I've heard about that," he replied, hesitantly. "But do you have an office here in the city?"

"Oh, we have many offices. We have offices up and down the state. In fact, we're national: we have at least one office in every state of the union, including Alaska and Hawaii."

He had this puzzled look on his face. He was searching his mind to identify this huge company he *must* have read or heard about, perhaps in his *Wall Street Journal*.

"As a matter of fact, we've gone international. And Management has a plan to put at least one office in every country of the world by the end of this business era."

I paused.

"Do you have that in your business?" I asked.

"Well, no. Not yet," he answered. "But you mentioned management. How do they make it work?"

"It's a family concern. There's a Father and a Son. . . . And they run everything."

"It must take a lot of capital," he asked, skeptically.

"You mean money?" I asked. "Yes, I suppose so. No one knows just how much it takes, but we never worry because there's never a shortage. The Boss always seems to have enough. He's a very creative guy. . . . And the money is, well, just there. In fact those of us in the Organization have a saying about our Boss: 'He owns the cattle on a thousand hills.'"

"Oh, he's into ranching too?" asked my captive friend.

"No, it's just a saying we use to indicate his wealth."

My friend sat back in his seat, musing over our conversation. "What about with you?" he asked.

"The employees? They are something to see," I said. "They have a 'Spirit' that pervades the organization. It works like this: the Father and Son love each other so much that their love filters down through the organization so that we all find ourselves loving one another too. I know this sounds old-fashioned in a world like ours, but I know people in the organization who are willing to die for me. Do you have that in your business?" I was almost shouting now. People were starting to shift noticeably in their seats.

"Not yet," he said. Quickly changing strategies, he asked, "But do you have good benefits?"

"They're substantial," I countered, with a gleam. "I have complete life insurance, fire insurance — all the basics. You might not believe this, but it's true I have holdings in a mansion that's being built for me right now for my retirement. Do you have that in your business?"

"Not yet," he answered, wistfully. The light was dawning.

"You know, one thing bothers me about all you're saying. I've read the journals, and if your business is all you say it is, why haven't I heard about it before now?"

"That's a good question," I said. "After all, we have a 2000-year-old tradition."

"Wait a minute!" he said.

"You're right," I interrupted. "I'm talking about the church."

"I knew it. You know, I'm Jewish."

"Want to sign up?" I asked. [9]

We've all been there, haven't we? Most of us are not as creative as the minister, however. We just stumble through a few words and hope the person soon changes the subject. We feel awkward.

Four Hindrances to Evangelism

When you analyze our lack of evangelistic success and skill, it boils down to four primary reasons.

1. Ignorance

We just don't know how to do it. We have no method or proven "technique" that allows us to feel comfortable talking to others about Christ. We don't like a canned approach so we wind up with no approach.

2. Fear

Most of us are just plain scared. We're afraid the person will ask us a question we can't answer. Or he or she may become angry and tell us off.

3. Indifference

Hard as it is to admit it, many Christians just don't care. We think, "If that's the way the person wants to believe, that's fine. To each his own."

4. Bad Experience

More and more I meet believers who were turned off during their non-Christian years by some wild-eyed fanatic who pushed and embarrassed them, trying to force a decision. The result? A reluctance to say *anything* at all.

One Major Principle to Remember

If it's possible, let's set aside all those excuses and start from scratch. In fact, let's start *below* scratch. There is one principle that has helped me more than any other. It never fails to rescue me from dumb mistakes, and when I forget to employ it, I suffer the consequences. Here it is:

PUT YOURSELF IN THE OTHER PERSON'S PLACE.

If we can keep in mind that the person is not coming from where we are, nor does he or she understand where we are going, it will help greatly. Not infrequently will we encounter people who have an entirely different mindset or cultural background from ours, thus adding immeasurably to the complication. Jim Petersen, with The Navigators in Brazil, tells of witnessing to a well-educated industrial chemist named Osvaldo. Jim had been studying the Bible with the man's brother, and Osvaldo was curious about why his brother became so interested. Jim attempted to answer the chemist's questions by explaining the gospel to him.

> I got a piece of chalk and a Bible and used the wooden floor as a chalkboard. I spent the next two hours showing him a favorite diagram I often used to explain the message. I was quite satisfied with my performance, and when I

finally finished, I leaned back to observe his reaction, certain he would be on the verge of repentance.

Instead, he gazed at my illustration, then at me. He was puzzled. "Do you mean to tell me that this is why you came all the way to Brazil, to tell people that?" he said.

To Osvaldo, what I had said seemed insignificant and irrelevant. I recognized at that moment that I was facing a communication problem I had never been aware of before. [10]

Jim was wise not to argue or push. He was honest enough to realize the man wasn't being argumentative... he was just coming from another frame of reference. Those who cultivate the skill of evangelism do their best to put themselves inside the other person's skin. They do this by thinking thoughts like:

"Please think about what I'm saying. Don't just expect me to listen, you listen, too."

"If you want me to hear you, scratch my itches."

"Talk with me — don't talk down to me."

"Make sense. No riddles or secret religious code words, okay?"

Six Guidelines
Worth Remembering

All of this leads us to an account in the New Testament where one man witnessed to another with remarkable success—because he did so with wisdom and skill. I never cease to marvel at the beautiful way God used him to reach out to a person (a total stranger!) from another culture and graciously guide the man to faith in Jesus Christ.

The story is found in Acts 8, a story that begins in the midst of an exciting revival, much like one that sweeps across a city during a Billy Graham Crusade. In Acts 8 the territory where revival fires are spreading is Samaria.

> So, when they had solemnly testified and spoken the word of the Lord, they started back to Jerusalem, and were preaching the gospel to many villages of the Samaritans. (Acts 8:25)

There was renewed enthusiasm. Those bold Christians were proclaiming Christ from village to village. The Spirit of God was working. The atmosphere was electric. If you've ever been a part of a scene like this, you need no further explanation. If you haven't, you cannot imagine the excitement. A contagious, authentic enthusiasm ignites the souls of men and women with such spiritual fire it's almost frightening.

Suddenly God steps in and does something strange. Without prior announcement—out of the clear blue—He dispatches an angel from heaven and redirects a man named Philip.

> But an angel of the Lord spoke to Philip
> saying, "Get up and go south to the road
> that descends from Jerusalem to Gaza."
> (This is a desert road.) So he got up and
> went. (Acts 8:26–27)

I'd like us to remember several guidelines that relate to personal evangelism. Each one will help us hurdle the barriers and become skilled in sharing our faith. The first of six is found here at the beginning of this account.

Sensitivity

How easy it would have been for Philip to be so caught up in the excitement and electricity of that Samaritan revival—where God was obviously at work—that he wasn't sensitive to a new direction. Not this man! He was alert and ready. Each day marked a new beginning. He had walked with God long enough to know that He has the right to throw a surprise curve—*and often does!*

Without stating His reason, without revealing the ultimate plan, God led Philip away from Samaria and out onto a desert road. The man was so sensitive to God's leading there was no struggle. People who become skilled in sharing their faith possess this sensitivity to God.

Availability

With sensitivity comes availability. There's no use having a sensitive spirit if we are not available and willing to go . . . wherever. Take a look at the next episode in Philip's life:

> And there was an Ethiopian eunuch, a
> court official of Candace, queen of the
> Ethiopians, who was in charge of all her
> treasure; and he had come to Jerusalem
> to worship, and he was returning and

> sitting in his chariot, and was reading
> the prophet Isaiah. Then the Spirit said
> to Philip, "Go up and join this chariot."
> (Acts 8:27–29)

Like our pastor friend on the plane, Philip encountered a choice opportunity. Who was riding along that desert road? A political leader from the third world. The Secretary of the Treasury of the Candace Dynasty, no less! And where had he been? To church! But the Ethiopian official had not met the Lord—he had only had his curiosity aroused. But out there in the middle of the desert is this guy in a chariot reading the Scriptures. Don't tell me God can't pull it off! And of all places to be reading, the man is reading Isaiah 53, the seed plot of the gospel in the Old Testament. God says to His servant Philip, "Go for it . . . join up with that chariot!"

Those who are available experience exciting moments like this. It's thrilling to be a part of the irresistible momentum, caught in the current of the Spirit's working. Philip's obedience pays off. His heart must have begun to beat faster.

Initiative

Look at the next move Philip made:

> Philip ran up and heard him reading
> Isaiah the prophet, and said, "Do you
> understand what you are reading?"
> (Acts 8:30)

He took the initiative. But there is not a hint of offense or put down in his approach. Just simply, "Do you know what you are reading?" He genuinely wanted to know if the stranger in the chariot understood those words.

Initiative is so important. It is the first plank in the bridge-building process. But like the cornerstone, it must be placed very carefully. And the use of questions is an excellent approach. Here are a few I have used with a good deal of success:

> "Say, I've been reading a lot about our world lately. Do you have any idea what's gone wrong?"

> "I'm interested in the lives of great men and women. Who, in your opinion, was the greatest person who ever lived?"

> "With all these earthquakes and other calamities that happen so quickly, what keeps you from being afraid? Do you pray or something?"

Author Ann Kiemel asks, "Can I sing to you?" Now *that's* a creative starter! The late Paul Little was a master at taking the initiative. He mentions a few suggestions that I have found helpful.

> After even a vague reference to "religion" in a conversation, many Christians have used this practical series of questions to draw out latent spiritual interest: First, "By the way, are you interested in spiritual things?" Many will say, "Yes." But even if the person says, "No," we can ask a second question, "What do you think a real Christian is?" Wanting to hear his opinion invariably pleases a person. From his response we'll also gain a more accurate, first-hand—if perhaps shocking—understanding of his thinking as a non-Christian; and because we have listened to him he'll

be much more ready to listen to us. Answers to this question usually revolve around some external action — going to church, reading the Bible, praying, tithing, being baptized. After such an answer we can agree that a real Christian usually *does* these things, but then point out that that's not what a real Christian *is*. A real Christian is one who is personally related to Jesus Christ as a living Person.

The bait can also be thrown out succinctly if we are prepared for questions we are asked frequently. Often we recognize after it is too late that we have had a wonderful opportunity to speak up but we missed it because we didn't know what to say at the moment. Sometimes we are asked questions like: "Why are you so happy?" "What makes you tick?" "You seem to have a different motivation. You're not like me and most people. Why?" "Why is it you seem to have purpose in life?" Again, we can say, "An experience I had changed my outlook on life." And then, as we are asked, we can share that experience of Christ with them.[11]

Above all, take it easy. Proceed with caution. It's like fishing. Patience, intelligence, and skill are not optional. They're *essential*. No one ever caught fish by slapping the water with an oar or by hurriedly racing through the process. Taking the initiative requires that we do so with a lot of wisdom, which brings us to the fourth guideline.

Tactfulness

There is one very obvious observation regarding Philip's method I find extremely appealing. He was completely unoffensive. It is important for Christians to remember that it is the *cross* that will be offensive, *not the one who witnesses*. Philip used tact as he became involved in a discussion with the Ethiopian official.

> Philip ran up and heard him reading
> Isaiah the prophet, and said, "Do you
> understand what you are reading?"
> And he said, "Well, how could I, unless
> someone guides me?" And he invited
> Philip to come up and sit with him.
> Now the passage of Scripture which he
> was reading was this:
>
> > "He was led as a sheep to slaughter;
> > And as a lamb before its shearer
> >   is silent,
> > So He does not open His mouth.
> > In humiliation His judgment was
> >   taken away;
> > Who will relate His generation?
> > For His life is removed from the
> >   earth."
>
> The eunuch answered Philip and
> said, "Please tell me, of whom does
> the prophet say this? Of himself or of
> someone else?" (Acts 8:30–34).

He listened without responding as the man confessed his ignorance. He graciously awaited an invitation to climb up into the chariot before doing so. He started where the man was, rather than cranking out a canned sermon. Not once did Philip put the man down. Or pull rank. Or attempt to impress. He gave the stranger space to think it through without feeling foolish.

Rebecca Pippert, in her fine book on evangelism, *Out of the Salt Shaker and Into the World*, mentions the need for this approach:

> I remember a skeptical student who said, "I could never be a Christian. My commitment to scholarship makes any consideration of Christianity impossible. It's irrational and the evidence supporting it is totally insufficient."
>
> I answered, "I'm so glad you care so much about truth and that you really want evidence to support your beliefs. You say the evidence for Christianity is terribly insufficient. What was your conclusion after carefully investigating the primary biblical documents?"
>
> "Ahh, well, you mean the Bible?" he asked.
>
> "Of course," I said. "The New Testament accounts of Jesus, for example. Where did you find them lacking?"
>
> "Oh, well, look, I remember mother reading me those stories when I was ten," he replied.
>
> "Hmm, but what was your conclusion?" I continued and as a result discovered he had never investigated the Scriptures critically as an adult. This is all too often the case. But we can arouse curiosity in others to investigate the claims of the gospel when we help them

see that their information and understanding about Christianity is lacking.

Another person who was quite hostile to what she perceived was Christianity told me in anger, "I can't stand those hypocrites who go to church every Sunday. They make me sick."

"Yes," I responded, "isn't it amazing how far they are from true Christianity? When you think of how vast the difference is between the real thing and what they do, it's like worlds apart. Ever since I've discovered what Christianity is really about, the more mystified I am."

"Ah, the real thing? Well, what do you mean by that?" she asked. We talked for an hour about faith because her hostility had been changed into curiosity. [12]

Rather than arguing, try to find a way to agree. Rather than attacking, show genuine concern. Uphold the dignity of the individual. He or she may not be a Christian, but that is no reason to think the person lacks our respect. As questions are asked (like the Ethiopian asked in verse 34), kindly offer an answer. That man was a Gentile. He had no idea of whom Isaiah, the Jewish prophet, was speaking. Philip stayed calm and tactful. But when the moment was right, he came to the point.

Preciseness

In answer to the man's question, Philip spoke precisely and clearly of Jesus Christ, the Messiah:

> The eunuch answered Philip and
> said, "Please tell me, of whom does
> the prophet say this? Of himself or of
> someone else?"
>
> Then Philip opened his mouth,
> and beginning from this Scripture he
> preached Jesus to him. (Acts 8:34–35)

He started at square one—no mumbo-jumbo, no jargon, no double-talk, no scary charts of pyramids of multi-headed beasts or superaggressive "believe now or you'll go to hell" threats. Just *Jesus*—Jesus's person and work, Jesus's love for sinners, Jesus's perfect life and sacrificial death, Jesus's resurrection and offer of forgiveness, security, purpose, and hope. "He preached Jesus. . . ."

Stay on the issue of Christ when witnessing. Not the church or denominations or religion or theological differences or doctrinal questions. Speak precisely of Jesus, the Savior. Refuse to dart down rabbit trails. Satellite subjects are often tantalizingly tempting, but *refrain*! When self-control is applied, the other person will realize that the gospel revolves strictly around Christ and nothing else. See what happened?

> And Philip said, "If you believe with all
> your heart, you may." And he answered
> and said, "I believe that Jesus Christ is
> the Son of God."

And he ordered the chariot to stop;
and they both went down into the
water, Philip as well as the eunuch, and
he baptized him.

When they came up out of the
water, the Spirit of the Lord snatched
Philip away; and the eunuch no longer
saw him, but went on his way rejoicing.
(Acts 8:37–39)

Decisiveness

The African gentleman suggested that he be baptized. Wisely, Philip put first things first. With decisive discernment, Philip explained that faith in Jesus *precedes* baptism. That did it! The man believed and was *then* baptized. No ifs, ands, or buts. *First* there was an acceptance of the message and *after that* there was a public acknowledgment of his faith as he submitted to baptism.

Summary and Conclusion

Do you genuinely desire to strengthen your grip on evangelism? Are you honestly interested in sharing your faith with this generation of lost and confused people? Begin to cultivate these six guidelines:

- *Sensitivity*. Listen carefully. Be ready to follow God's leading.

- *Availability*. Stay flexible. If the Lord is directing you to move here or there, go.

- *Initiative*. Use an appropriate approach to break the ice.

- *Tactfulness.* With care and courtesy, with thoughtfulness, with a desire to uphold dignity, speak graciously.

- *Preciseness.* Remember the issue is Christ. Stay on that subject.

- *Decisiveness.* As the Spirit of God is evidently at work, speak of receiving Christ. Make it clear that Jesus Christ is ready to receive whomever may come to Him by faith.

I began this chapter with a statement evangelist Billy Graham once made. I close with the same question for emphasis.

> The evangelistic harvest is always urgent. The destiny of men and of nations is always being decided.
>
> Every generation is strategic. We are not responsible for the past generation, and we cannot bear the full responsibility for the next one; but we do have our generation. God will hold us responsible as to how well we fulfill our responsibilities to this age and take advantage of our opportunities. [13]

Because today's harvest is urgent, because we are held responsible to make Christ known to our generation, let's not allow our laid-back, who-really-cares society to weaken our enthusiasm or slacken our zeal.

Let's strengthen our grip on evangelism.

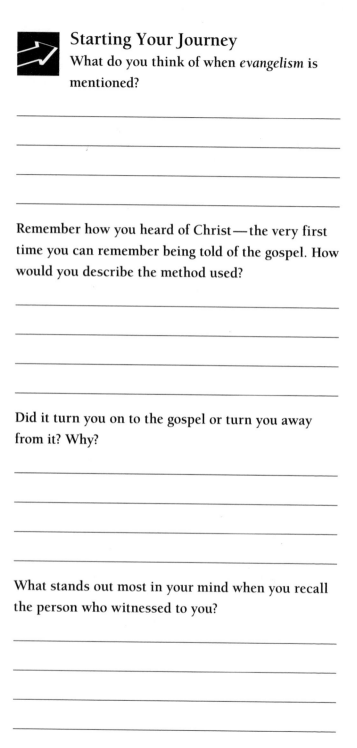

Starting Your Journey

What do you think of when *evangelism* is mentioned?

_____

_____

_____

_____

Remember how you heard of Christ—the very first time you can remember being told of the gospel. How would you describe the method used?

_____

_____

_____

_____

Did it turn you on to the gospel or turn you away from it? Why?

_____

_____

_____

_____

What stands out most in your mind when you recall the person who witnessed to you?

_____

_____

_____

_____

We worked our way fairly carefully through a section of Acts 8 in this chapter. Turn to those verses (8:26–40) and see if you can remember a few of the guidelines. Can you recall all six of them in order?

1. _____
_____

2. _____
_____

3. _____
_____

4. _____
_____

5. _____
_____

6. _____
_____

Pick one from the list and mull it over; discuss it with others if you're working in a group. Why is this so significant that you chose it over all the others?

_____
_____
_____
_____

If you were to instruct others on the do's and don'ts of evangelism based on this chapter and your own experiences, how would you advise them? Complete the following chart and then discuss this with the people in your group.

**Things to Guard Against
(The Negative Turn-offs)**

**Things to Remember
(The Positive Approaches)**

During the coming week, *pray* that you might be sensitive to at least one opportunity to witness. Think about what you want to communicate ahead of time. As the occasion occurs, *speak* graciously and carefully. Finally, be ready to *ask* the person if he or she would wish to receive the gift of eternal life. Then share your experience with other believers.

My Questions and Thoughts

My Questions and Thoughts

Chapter 3

Tools for Evangelism

One of the most powerful tools you can use to explain
the gospel is a simple diagram. You can sketch it
anywhere—on a napkin at a restaurant, in the sand at
the beach, or on the back of a business card. Take a few
moments to study it, and be sure to look up the verses
and slip them into your memory.

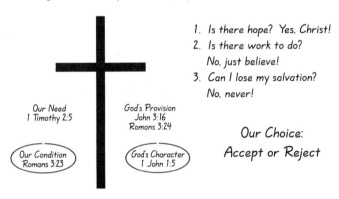

1. Is there hope? Yes, Christ!
2. Is there work to do?
   No, just believe!
3. Can I lose my salvation?
   No, never!

Our Need
1 Timothy 2:5

God's Provision
John 3:16
Romans 3:24

Our Condition
Romans 3:23

God's Character
1 John 1:5

Our Choice:
Accept or Reject

Do you think you can talk your way through this
diagram? Try following this procedure:

On a separate piece of paper, begin by sketching
the circle on the left and writing, "Our Condition,
Romans 3:23." Review this verse, and summarize it in
your own words.

Next, draw the other circle, and write, "God's
Character, 1 John 1:5." Again, summarize this verse
as simply as you can. To help the person visualize the

barrier between us and God, draw the vertical line of the cross between the two circles.

Sketch the arrow that goes from left to right, and write, "Our Need, 1 Timothy 2:5." Using this verse, describe its meaning in one sentence.

Finally, pencil in the arrow that goes from right to left, and finish the cross by drawing the horizontal line. Write, "God's Provision, John 3:16; Romans 3:24." Review these verses, and restate them in your own words.

After you finish explaining what Christ has accomplished for us on the cross, write down the three questions, answering them one at a time. Conclude by writing, "Our Choice: Accept or Reject." Your purpose is not to manipulate a decision, but simply to lay out the fact that the gospel requires a response. Either we believe it or we don't.

Some people may not be ready to accept Christ, and yet they may not be willing to reject Him either. God never forces His grace on anyone, and neither should we. However, we can help the person see that choosing not to accept Him is really the same as rejecting Him. There is no middle ground.

If the person needs time to think, give him plenty of room. Before concluding your time together, perhaps ask him if he can pinpoint what issue or question is holding him back. Sometimes talking about it will help him resolve it. You may also wish to put into his hands one of these books: *Who Is This Jesus?* by Michael Green (Nashville: Thomas Nelson Publishers, 1992) or *Reason to Believe: A Response to Common Objections to Christianity* by R. C. Sproul (Grand Rapids: Zondervan, 1982).

If the person is ready to accept Christ, that's wonderful! You may encourage your friend to express his decision to the Lord in prayer. There's no magic formula for this prayer. The thief on the cross simply cried out, "Jesus, remember me when You come in Your kingdom!" (Luke 23:42). If your friend needs help, you may use the following prayer as a guide:

> Dear God,
>
> I know that my sin has put a barrier between You and me. Thank You for sending Jesus to die in my place. I accept Your gift of eternal life and ask Jesus to be my personal Savior. Please begin to guide my life. Thank You. In Jesus's name, amen.

Never underestimate the power of the gospel. It can change a person's life — forever.

Common Questions: Dealing with Issues of Faith and Spiritual Growth

Q: Why should I believe the Bible? How do I know that it's true?

A: We believe the Bible because it's God's inspired Word, it claims to be true, and it proves itself to be true in the lives of believers. Paul wrote in 1 Thessalonians 2:13:

> For this reason we also constantly thank God that when you received the word of God which you heard from us, you accepted it not as the word of men, but for what it really is, the word of God, which also performs its work in you who believe.

The prophet Isaiah calls God "the God of truth" in Isaiah 65:16. Our Father reveals His truth to us primarily through the Bible. In Matthew 4:4, Jesus attested to the truth and authority of Scripture when He said, "Man shall not live on bread alone, but on every word that proceeds out of the mouth of God." The psalmist also testified to the veracity of Scripture:

> You are near, O LORD,
> And all Your commandments are truth.
> (Psalm 119:151)

> The sum of Your word is truth,
> And every one of Your righteous ordinances is everlasting. (Psalm 119:160)

God has no intention of hiding His perfect truth from the people He so lovingly created. He desires for every person on earth "to come to the knowledge of the truth" (1 Timothy 2:4), so He reveals His truth to us through His Word. The fact that He is truth guarantees that He will reveal Himself as He really is, that His revelation will be perfectly reliable, that what He says will correspond exactly to the way things are. At least four times in Scripture, we're assured that God does not lie (Numbers 23:19; 1 Samuel 15:29; Titus 1:2; and Hebrews 6:18). When the Almighty speaks, His words are true and accurate.

Q: I understand that Jesus Christ is much more than just a "great moral teacher," but how do I know that He's the true Messiah prophesied about in Scripture?

A: We can look back at Old Testament prophecies and discern two distinct lines of prophecy regarding the coming of the Messiah. One line predicted the first coming of the Messiah as the suffering Savior who would redeem His people by dying on the cross and then rising from the dead (Psalm 22; Isaiah 52:13–53:12). The other line of prophecy foretold the eternal kingdom that the Messiah would establish after He had atoned for the sins of His people (Isaiah 9:6–7; Daniel 7:13–14).

These two prophecies concerning the Messiah were not fully understood by the Old Testament saints, but we understand them now because of the testimonies of the gospel writers and the explanation of prophecies by the apostle Paul. When the Lord Jesus Christ presented Himself to the nation of Israel, He did so as their promised Messiah. In Luke chapter 4, He presented Himself as the fulfillment of Isaiah's prophecy (Isaiah 61:1–2). By His works, Jesus validated His power and authority to make such a claim. By His teaching, He revealed the true nature of His Messiahship and His eternal kingdom.

However, most Israelites had a different kind of Messiah in mind. They sought a Messiah of earthly magnificence, awesome power, and military might rather than one of humility who emptied Himself of glory to come to earth, take on human flesh, and die to save us from our sins (Philippians 2:5–8). Consequently, some people began to withdraw from Christ, and the Jewish leadership in His day quickly began to resist Him as a threat to their concept of who the Messiah "should be."

None of this caught Christ by surprise. He knew that He must first suffer before He could reign. Jesus began to withdraw from ministry to the masses and to pour His life into His disciples. He began to teach the crowds in the mysterious, veiled language of parables. He spoke less about His earthly kingdom and more about His plan for the church. He dealt less with Jews and more with Gentiles. He rebuked the Jewish leaders more openly, revealing their error. He even willingly submitted to the Father's plan and accepted death by the hands of His opponents—just as the Scriptures predicted the Messiah would do.

The Bible records and supports the authentication of Jesus Christ as Israel's Messiah, as well as His presentation of Himself as the Son of God and His rejection by His own people. All of these events fulfill the Old Testament prophecies concerning the Messiah and confirm that Jesus truly was the long-awaited One referred to in the Old Testament Scriptures.

Q: Is Jesus the only way to God? If so, how do we know?

A: Many passages of Scripture confirm that God has made salvation available to us by faith alone—faith in the birth, death, and resurrection of His Son, Jesus Christ, and the eternal, abundant life that He offers us. Probably the best-known passage supporting this truth is John 14:6, where Jesus says to Thomas, "I am the way, and the truth, and the life; no one comes to the Father but through Me." Other supporting passages are:

> God has given us eternal life, and this life is in His Son. He who has the Son has the life; he who does not have the Son of God does not have the life. (1 John 5:11–12)

> He [Jesus] is the stone which was rejected by you, the builders, but which became the chief corner stone. And there is salvation in no one else; for there is no other name under heaven that has been given among men by which we must be saved. (Acts 4:11–12)

> If you confess with your mouth Jesus
> as Lord, and believe in your heart that
> God raised Him from the dead, you will
> be saved; for with the heart a person
> believes, resulting in righteousness, and
> with the mouth he confesses, resulting
> in salvation. (Romans 10:9–10)

Christ came to earth, died, and rose again to offer us salvation. We believe God's Word to be true, and we experience the truth of Scripture's words, its claims, and its principles in our daily lives. Scripture claims that Christ is the only way to salvation; God claims that Christ is the only way; Jesus Himself claims in no uncertain terms that He is the only way; and the apostles and saints have affirmed throughout history that Jesus is the only way. If these claims are true, then the contradictory claims of other religions and philosophies that *they* are the only way (or alternative ways) to reach the same goal must be false. Jesus Himself taught that "the gate is small and the way is narrow that leads to life, and there are few who find it" (Matthew 7:14).

Christ is the only doorway to salvation, but the door's wide open! God wants every person to come to Him in faith, claiming redemption through Christ. The apostle Peter wrote in 2 Peter 3:9, "The Lord is not slow about His promise, as some count slowness, but is patient toward you, not wishing for any to perish but for all to come to repentance." Once we have chosen to walk through the door of salvation, we have the privilege of graciously sharing our message with others who may not realize or understand that Christ is the *only* way to God.

Q: I recently attended a church where the pastor taught that a person must be baptized by immersion before he or she can be truly saved. Is this true? What does the Bible say?

A: If we say that a person has to be baptized to be saved, we are adding something to the *only* prerequisite the Bible requires of a person for salvation: *faith*. The apostle Paul used Abraham as the leading example of one who was saved by grace through faith alone—before the rite of circumcision, before the Old Testament Law (Romans 4:9–13).

More specifically, the New Testament teaches the ordinance of "believer's baptism." One who has believed in Christ may be baptized to signify his or her faith (Acts 10:47; 11:17; 19:1–5). In every biblical context where water baptism is mentioned along with belief, faith always precedes the ordinance (1 Peter 3:21).

In biblical contexts where baptism is included in the proclamation of the gospel, the inclusion of the ordinance of baptism only indicates a public transfer of allegiance to Christ. For example, Peter's command in Acts 2:38, "be baptized in the name of Jesus Christ for the forgiveness of your sins," is often misapplied in the church today. Peter gave the sermon in a context of Jews who would have understood baptism as a *proof* of faith—not a *part* of faith. Most of us in America have no qualms about being baptized in public. But in many other countries today, the meaning of water baptism is much more similar to what it was in Acts 2—a testimony to the community and to the world. It represents a complete break from the past. And it is common for newly baptized Christians to be arrested, spend time in jail, lose their family—or even lose their lives for the sake of the gospel.

Q: Why do so many unbelievers experience health, wealth, success, and happiness when they're not honoring God? Is God rewarding them?

A: King Solomon concluded that life apart from God is boring, empty, profitless, and purposeless. Yet all of us have encountered unbelievers and even atheists who appear to experience happiness and excitement in life. Does that contradict Solomon's conclusions?

The truth is that unbelievers and the ungodly will experience temporary enjoyment in life, even apart from a saving relationship with Christ. This is due to the gift of *common grace*, defined as "grace that is available to all humanity. Its benefits are experienced by all human beings without discrimination. It reaches out in a multitude of ways, promoting what is good and restraining what is evil." [14] Our loving Heavenly Father extends a certain grace even to those who reject Him and His gift of eternal life through His Son. Several forms of common grace include the revelation of God through nature (Romans 1:18–20), His provision of sunshine, rain, and crops in due season (Acts 14:16–17), ordered human government (Romans 13:1–2), and the presence of truth and beauty in the world (Philippians 4:8). [15]

Though unbelievers may experience some blessing and joy in the present, justice and wrath are stored up for them in eternity. In contrast, while believers experience the common effects of a sinful world now, in the world to come they will receive the full blessings of salvation.

Q: When I trust Christ, what can I expect will happen? Will I be the same or different? How will I know?

A: When we make the crucial decision to trust Jesus Christ as our Savior, two vital changes take place.

First of all, something happens deep *within* us. According to 2 Corinthians 5:17, we become an entirely new creation. We gain new motivations and new interests. Our interests begin to shift from ourselves to others—from the things of the flesh to the things of God. And a new group of people appears on the horizon of our lives—other Christians. We begin to be more vulnerable, more open, and more willing to confess our sin. Our desire to hide from God changes to a desire to spend more time with Him. Why? We become new creatures within.

Second, something happens *to* us. When we express our faith in Christ, we instantaneously enter the family of God. We may not feel any different at that exact moment, but something vital happens the moment we believe. We become a part of God's family forever.

When we choose to trust God, we become new creatures, and we join God's family. And those two things never change!

Q: I'm confused about the "sin nature" that I often hear other Christians talking about. After I became a Christian, did I lose my sin nature? If not, then what separates me as a believer from non-Christians?

A: The marvelous working of God in the life of a believer begins at the point of faith in Christ. The Bible speaks of a believer's life before Christ as the "old self," while the "new self" represents a Christian's spiritual rebirth. However, the apostle Paul's teaching that the "old self was crucified" with Christ (Romans 6:6) and yet still exists as something that we as believers must choose to "lay aside" (Ephesians 4:22) has led to some misunderstanding about what we call our "old nature" and our "new nature."

This confusion stems, in part, from a vague understanding of the term *nature*. The expression never refers specifically to a person or thing, but to the *qualities* or *characteristics* of a person or thing. For example, Jesus has two natures—human and divine—eternally joined in one person. While He lived on earth, Christ expressed both His humanity and divinity as one man. His dual natures existed in perfect harmony. Our "sinful nature" and our "saintly nature," on the other hand, do not.

From one perspective, we have two natures because the attributes of both sin and righteousness remain within us, and these two natures are at war with one another (Romans 7:15–25). But from another perspective, God sees us with all "old things passed away" (2 Corinthians 5:17)—as people who now have righteous standing through the death and resurrection of Christ. Because Scripture teaches aspects of both perspectives, we cannot make them mutually exclusive.

Christ has "done away with" (or literally, "made powerless") our sinful nature (Romans 6:6). This doesn't mean the sinful nature no longer exists, but *it no longer has the power to make us sin*. The fact that Christians now find their identity in Christ alone does not mean the old, sinful nature no longer exerts its influence on us. It only means we don't have to respond to it because we have the power of the Holy Spirit to help us overcome the temptation to sin.

Q: I've prayed over and over again for God to take away a particular sin in my life, but I keep falling into the same sin. Does this mean that my heart hasn't truly been changed?

A: While we as believers will still commit some sins after we accept Christ, our lives should not be carnal or controlled by negative sin patterns. We're no longer in bondage to sin or to our fleshly desires. God has granted us the ability to exercise wisdom, discernment, self-control, and discipline as the Holy Spirit guides our thoughts, words, and actions.

Knowing Scripture, being accountable to others, and practicing daily spiritual disciplines are some of the best ways to arm yourself against dangerous sin patterns. The daily practice of the spiritual life is part of the means by which believers are able to more intimately know their God, relate to and rest in their new life in Christ, and experience true spiritual change and liberation from life-dominating patterns of sin. The spiritual disciplines promote growth in our devotion to God and our ability to grasp, personalize, believe, and apply Scripture to our lives.

Assembling together weekly with other believers for accountability, fellowship, worship, ministry, prayer, and the teaching of God's Word is also vital to our spiritual health. The Holy Spirit does not operate in a mindless vacuum devoid of God's point of view. The Word and the Spirit work together, so that if we fail to take time to get alone with God and His Word two things will happen: we will quench the ministry of the Spirit, and we will be influenced and deceived by the negative attitudes and ungodly viewpoints of the world around us.

Our heavenly Father may allow *trials* in our lives, but He will never *tempt* us to sin. James wrote:

> Let no one say when he is tempted,
> "I am being tempted by God"; for God
> cannot be tempted by evil, and He
> Himself does not tempt anyone. But
> each one is tempted when he is carried
> away and enticed by his own lust. Then
> when lust has conceived, it gives birth
> to sin; and when sin is accomplished, it
> brings forth death. (James 1:13–15)

See the progression? Sin and temptation are part of an insidious process by which our fleshly lusts and desires lead to sin, and our sin, ultimately, leads to spiritual death. But God's power triumphs over both Satan's power and the power of our own desires. God's Word promises us that,

> No temptation has overtaken you but
> such as is common to man; and God is
> faithful, who will not allow you to be
> tempted beyond what you are able, but
> with the temptation will provide the
> way of escape also, so that you will be
> able to endure it. (1 Corinthians 10:13)

Paul wrote, "If anyone is in Christ, he is a new creature; the old things passed away; behold, new things have come" (2 Corinthians 5:17). When we look at the delicate finery of a butterfly's wings, we find it hard to believe that this exquisite creature was once a fat, ugly caterpillar crawling around in the dirt. You've experienced spiritual metamorphosis; you're a new creature. Are you living like it?

Q: Is it possible to do something that would cause me to lose my salvation?

A: Romans 8:38–39 says that no "created thing" can separate us from the love of God, given to us through Jesus Christ. Because you and I are "created thing[s]," Paul states very strongly that under no circumstance could we ever do something that would cause us to lose our salvation.

Earlier in the same chapter of Romans, Paul says that "these whom [God] justified, He also glorified" (8:30). From our perspective, we have not yet been glorified; that will not happen in this life. But from God's perspective, it's already done. Our salvation is complete in His sight, including the initial moment of salvation called *justification*, the ongoing work of salvation called *sanctification*, and the final work of salvation called *glorification*. What greater assurance do we need that God would not under any circumstance undo the work which He has already completed? Jesus affirmed this truth in John 10:27–28: "My sheep hear My voice, and I know them, and they follow Me; and I give eternal life to them, and they will never perish; and no one will snatch them out of My hand."

Resources for Probing Further

For those who want to probe further into the topic of evangelism, we recommend the following resources written by or edited by Bible-believing scholars.

Evangelism Foundations

Aldrich, Joe. *Lifestyle Evangelism: Learning to Open Your Life to Those Around You.* Portland, Ore.: Multnomah, 1999.

Coleman, Robert E. *The Master Plan of Evangelism.* Reprint. Grand Rapids: Fleming H. Revell, 2006.

Pippert, Rebecca Manley. *Out of the Saltshaker and into the World: Evangelism as a Way of Life.* Rev. and exp. ed. Downers Grove, Ill.: InterVarsity, 1999.

Evangelism How-Tos

Aldrich, Joseph C. *Gentle Persuasion: Creative Ways to Introduce Your Friends to Christ.* Portland, Ore.: Multnomah, 1988.

Jacks, Bob, Betty Jacks, and Ron Wormser, Sr. *Your Home a Lighthouse: Hosting an Evangelistic Bible Study.* Rev. ed. Colorado Springs: NavPress, 1987.

Kramp, John. *Out of Their Faces and into Their Shoes: How to Understand Spiritually Lost People and Give Them Directions to God.* Nashville: Broadman & Holman, 1995.

Little, Paul E. *How to Give Away Your Faith.* Rev. and Updated ed. Downers Grove, Ill.: InterVarsity, 2006.

Petersen, Jim. *Living Proof: Sharing the Gospel Naturally.* Colorado Springs: NavPress, 1989.

Evangelism Resources for Pastors

Barna, George. *Evangelism That Works: How to Reach Changing Generations With the Unchanging Gospel.* Ventura, Calif.: Regal Books, 1995.

Loscalzo, Craig A. *Evangelistic Preaching That Connects: Guidance in Shaping Fresh & Appealing Sermons.* Downers Grove, Ill.: InterVarsity, 1995.

Search Ministries. 5038 Dorsey Hall Drive, Ellicott City, MD 21042. (410) 740-5300. www.searchnational.org. This ministry provides evangelism training and consulting as well as the excellent *Common Ground* bulletin insert.

Evangelism Tracts and Publications

Steps to Peace with God (Billy Graham, www.billygraham.org)

The Four Spiritual Laws (Campus Crusade for Christ, www.ccci.org)

The Bridge to Life (NavPress, www.navpress.com)

May I Ask You a Question? (EvanTell, www.evantell.org)

Resources to Follow Evangelism

Swindoll, Charles R. *The Grace Awakening.* Nashville: W Publishing Group, 2003.

Swindoll, Charles R. *Growing Deep in the Christian Life: Essential Truths for Becoming Strong in the Faith.* Grand Rapids: Zondervan, 1995.

Swindoll, Charles R. *Perfect Trust.* Nashville: J. Countryman, 2000.

Swindoll, Charles R. *So, You Want to Be Like Christ? Eight Essentials to Get You There.* Nashville: W Publishing Group, 2005.

Swindoll, Charles R. *So, You Want to Be Like Christ? Eight Essentials to Get You There Workbook*. Nashville: W Publishing Group, 2005.

Swindoll, Charles R. *Start Where You Are: Catch a Fresh Vision for Your Life*. Nashville: W Publishing Group, 1999.

Swindoll, Charles R. *Strengthening Your Grip: How to Live Confidently in an Aimless World*. Nashville: W Publishing Group, 1998.

How to Begin a Relationship with God

The Bible is the most marvelous book in the world, and it is the true Life-Map that marks the path to God. This map not only tells us how to avoid pitfalls and how to navigate the sudden roadblocks in life, but it also reveals how to enjoy the journey to the fullest. How? It points us to God—our ultimate destination. It tells us how we can come to know God Himself. Let's look at four vital truths the Scripture reveals.

Our Spiritual Condition: Totally Corrupt

The first truth is rather personal. One look in the mirror of Scripture, and our human condition becomes painfully clear:

> There is none righteous, not even one;
> There is none who understands,
> There is none who seeks for God;
> All have turned aside, together they
>   have become useless;
> There is none who does good,
> There is not even one.
> (Romans 3:10–12)

We are all sinners through and through—totally depraved. Now, that doesn't mean we've committed every atrocity known to humankind. We're not as *bad* as we can be, just as *bad off* as we can be. Sin colors all of our thoughts, motives, words, and actions.

You still don't believe it? Look around. Everything around us bears the smudge marks of our sinful nature. Despite our best efforts to create a perfect world, crime statistics continue to soar, divorce rates keep climbing, and families keep crumbling.

Something has gone terribly wrong in our society and in ourselves—something deadly. Contrary to how the world would repackage it, "me-first" living doesn't equal rugged individuality and freedom; it equals death. As Paul said in his letter to the Romans, "The wages of sin is death" (Romans 6:23)—our spiritual and physical death that comes from God's righteous judgment of our sin, along with all of the emotional and practical effects of this separation that we experience on a daily basis. This brings us to the second truth: God's character.

God's Character: Infinitely Holy

How can a good and just God judge us for a sinful nature into which we were born? Our total depravity is only half the answer. The other half is God's infinite holiness.

The fact that we know things are not as they should be points us to a standard of goodness beyond ourselves. Our sense of injustice in life on this side of eternity implies a perfect standard of justice beyond our reality. That standard and source is God Himself. And God's standard of holiness contrasts starkly with our sinful condition.

Scripture says that "God is Light, and in Him there is no darkness at all" (1 John 1:5). He is absolutely holy, which creates a problem for us. If He is so pure, how can we who are so impure relate to Him?

Perhaps we could try being better people, try to tilt the balance in favor of our good deeds, or seek out methods for self-improvement. Throughout history, people have attempted to live up to God's standard by keeping the Ten Commandments or living by their own code of ethics. Unfortunately, no one can come close to satisfying the demands of God's law. Romans 3:20 says, "By the works of the Law no flesh will be justified in His sight; for through the Law comes the knowledge of sin."

Our Need: A Substitute

So here we are, sinners by nature and sinners by choice, trying to pull ourselves up by our own bootstraps to attain a relationship with our holy Creator. But every time we try, we fall flat on our faces. We can't live a good enough life to make up for our sin, because God's standard isn't "good enough"—it's *perfection*. And we can't make amends for the offense our sin has created without dying for it.

Who can get us out of this mess?

If someone could live perfectly, honoring God's law, and would bear sin's death penalty for us—in our place—then we would be saved from our predicament. But is there such a person? Thankfully, yes!

Meet your substitute—*Jesus Christ*. He is the One who took death's place for you!

> [God] made [Jesus Christ] who
> knew no sin to be sin on our
> behalf, so that we might become the
> righteousness of God in Him.
> (2 Corinthians 5:21)

God's Provision: A Savior

God rescued us by sending His Son, Jesus, to die on the cross for our sins (1 John 4:9–10). Jesus was fully human and fully divine (John 1:1, 18), a truth that ensures His understanding of our weaknesses, His power to forgive, and His ability to bridge the gap between God and us (Romans 5:6–11). In short, we are "justified as a gift by His grace through the redemption which is in Christ Jesus" (Romans 3:24). Two words in this verse bear further explanation: *justified* and *redemption*.

Justification is God's act of mercy, in which He declares believing sinners righteous while they are still in their sinning state. Justification doesn't mean that God *makes* us righteous, so that we never sin again, rather that He *declares* us righteous—much like a judge pardons a guilty criminal. Because Jesus took our sin upon Himself and suffered our judgment on the cross, God forgives our debt and proclaims us PARDONED.

Redemption is God's act of paying the ransom price to release us from our bondage to sin. Held hostage by Satan, we were shackled by the iron chains of sin and death. Like a loving parent whose child has been kidnapped, God willingly paid the ransom for you. And what a price He paid! He gave His only Son to bear our sins—past, present, and future. Jesus's death and resurrection broke our chains and set us free to become children of God (Romans 6:16–18, 22; Galatians 4:4–7).

Placing Your Faith in Christ

These four truths describe how God has provided a way to Himself through Jesus Christ. Because the price has been paid in full by God, we must respond to His free gift of eternal life in total faith and confidence in Him to save us. We must step forward into the relationship with God that He has prepared for us—not by doing good works or by being good people, but by coming to Him just as we are and accepting His justification and redemption by faith.

> For by grace you have been saved through faith; and that not of your-selves, it is the gift of God; not as a result of works, so that no one may boast. (Ephesians 2:8–9)

We accept God's gift of salvation simply by placing our faith in Christ alone for the forgiveness of our sins. Would you like to enter into a relationship with your Creator by trusting in Christ as your Savior? If so, here's a simple prayer you can use to express your faith:

> *Dear God,*
>
> *I know that my sin has put a barrier between You and me. Thank You for sending Your Son, Jesus, to die in my place. I trust in Jesus alone to forgive my sins, and I accept His gift of eternal life. I ask Jesus to be my personal Savior and the Lord of my life. Thank You. In Jesus's name I pray, amen.*

If you've prayed this prayer or one like it and you wish to find out more about knowing God and His plan for you in the Bible, contact us at Insight for Living. You can speak to one of our pastors or women's counselors on staff by calling (972) 473-5097. Or you can write us at the address below.

Pastoral Ministries Department
Insight for Living
Post Office Box 269000
Plano, Texas 75026-9000

The next time you study a road map, remember the One who created the perfect plan for your life, and remind yourself that you know Him personally. Rejoice in His indescribable gift!

*I*nsight for *L*iving's
*E*ssential *B*eliefs

At Insight for Living, we affirm the following essential
beliefs:

The Bible — *We affirm our confidence in God's inerrant
Word. We treasure its truths, and we respect its reproofs.*

The 66 books of the Old and New Testaments are the
Word of God, inspired by the Holy Spirit, and written
over the centuries by chosen men of God. The Bible is
without error in its original manuscripts, is completely
reliable as the final authority in all matters of doctrine
and practice, and is centered on the person and work of
Jesus Christ. See 1 Thessalonians 2:13; 2 Timothy 3:15–17;
and 2 Peter 1:20–21.

God the Father — *We acknowledge the Creator-God as our
heavenly Father, infinitely perfect and intimately acquainted
with all our ways.*

There is one eternal, all-powerful, all-knowing, holy,
just, loving, true, and unchangeable God. However,
in the unity of the one God, there are three divine
persons — Father, Son, and Holy Spirit — equal in power
but distinct in roles. As the first person of the Trinity,
the Father is the source and ruler of all things and is
fatherly in His relationship with creation in general and
believers in particular. See Psalm 103:19; Matthew 28:19;
and 1 Peter 1:2.

The Lord Jesus Christ—*We claim Jesus Christ as our Lord—the very God who came in human flesh—the object of our worship and the subject of our praise.*

As the second person of the Trinity, the Son reveals the Father. According to the Father's plan, the eternal Son humbled Himself and became incarnate, inseparably uniting undiminished deity with true humanity. As fully God and fully man, Jesus Christ lived a sinless life, died to pay in full our penalty for sin, rose bodily and miraculously from the dead, ascended into heaven, and will come again in glory. See John 1:1–3, 14; Philippians 2:5–8; Hebrews 1:1–3; and 1 John 5:11–12.

The Holy Spirit—*We recognize the Holy Spirit as the third member of the Godhead who is incessantly at work convicting, convincing, and comforting.*

As the third person of the Trinity, the Holy Spirit is the personal agent of the Father and Son for revelation and regeneration. Though pervasively present and active in creation, the Holy Spirit specially dwells among God's people and uniquely indwells individual believers, giving them new life and empowering them for lives of personal holiness. See John 14:26; Acts 1:5, 8; 1 Corinthians 6:19–20; and Ephesians 1:13–14.

The Depravity of Humanity—*We confess that Adam's fall into sin left humanity without the hope of heaven apart from a new birth made possible by the Savior's substitutionary death and bodily resurrection.*

As a result of Adam's rebellion, all people have fallen under the curse of death. Unable and unwilling to please God, all humans are undeserving of His blessings, blinded to His truth, and dead in their sins—spiritually and, ultimately, physically. This state of judgment before the just and holy God is a condition that permeates every facet of human life and cannot be cured apart from the grace of God through Christ. See Genesis 3; Jeremiah 17:9; and Romans 3:10–18, 23; 5:12.

Salvation — *We believe the offer of salvation is God's love-gift to all. Those who accept it by faith, apart from works, become new creatures in Christ.*

Because fallen humans are unable to save themselves, God, according to His own sovereign mercy, acts to save those who come to Him by grace through faith. God sent His Son, Jesus Christ, to suffer the penalty of death in place of condemned humanity. Simply through believing the good news that Christ died for his or her sins and then rose from the dead, a person can be forgiven of all sin, declared righteous by God, reborn into new life, and guaranteed eternal life with God. See John 3:16; Romans 10:9–10; 1 Corinthians 15:1–5; and Ephesians 1:4–12; 2:8–9.

The Return of Christ — *We anticipate our Lord's promised return, which could occur at any moment.*

According to the Father's plan, Jesus Christ will one day return in power to bring completion of salvation and rewards to believers and judgment and wrath to unbelievers. The Bible teaches that the years leading up to the judgment will be marked by increasing evil, but the actual time of the end is unknown. It could begin at any moment. Though the details of Christ's return are sometimes unclear, its reality is certain, and all believers are called to live holy lives in anticipation of His coming. See 1 Thessalonians 4:13–5:11; 2 Thessalonians 2:1–12; Hebrews 9:28; and Revelation 19:11–16.

Resurrection of Humanity — *We are convinced that all who have died will be brought back from beyond — believers to everlasting communion with God and unbelievers to everlasting separation from God.*

Though a believer's spirit is ushered into the Lord's presence immediately upon physical death, the fullness of salvation awaits Christ's return, when He will resurrect believers in glorified bodies like His own immortal body which can never die. While all believers throughout history will enjoy eternal life in perfect paradise, unbelievers will be resurrected to suffer eternal conscious punishment for their sins. See John 11:23–27; 1 Corinthians 15:51–57; 1 Thessalonians 4:13–18; and Revelation 20:4–21:5.

The Body of Christ — *We know the Lord is continuing to enlarge His family, the universal body of Christ, over which He rules as head.*

The body of Christ is the ever-enlarging universal church consisting of true believers in heaven and on earth over whom Jesus Christ reigns as Lord. Regardless of denomination, all true believers are spiritually baptized by the Holy Spirit into Christ's body and are therefore spiritually united with Him and with one another. See Romans 12:4–5; 1 Corinthians 12:12–14; Ephesians 4:11–16; and 1 Peter 2:9–10.

The Family of God — *We are grateful to be a part of the local church, which exists to proclaim God's truth, to administer the ordinances, to stimulate growth toward maturity, and to bring glory to God.*

Believers are called to faithful membership in a visible, local congregation for the purpose of mutual encouragement and spiritual growth. As the family of God, a healthy local church is marked by God-glorifying worship, Scripture-centered teaching, intimate fellowship, and vivid expressions of the church's faith, hope, and love through evangelism, disciple-making, and service. See Acts 2:41–47; Philippians 2:1–4; and Hebrews 10:24–25.

$\mathcal{E}$ndnotes

1. Alister E. McGrath, *The Journey: A Pilgrim in the Lands of the Spirit*, 1st ed. (New York: Doubleday, 2000), 21–22.

2. Frank S. Mead, "Shepherd of the Senate," *Christian Herald*, November 1948.

3. Peter Marshall, "Mr. Jones, Meet the Master," in *Mr. Jones, Meet the Master*, ed. Catherine Marshall (New York: Fleming H. Revell, a division of Baker Publishing Group, 1950), 135–36. Used by permission.

4. Charles Wesley, "And Can It Be?" in *The Hymnal for Worship and Celebration* (Waco, Tex.: Word Music, 1986), 203.

5. Wesley, "And Can It Be?" 203.

6. Billy Graham, *How to Be Born Again* (Waco, Tex.: Word Books, a division of Thomas Nelson, Inc., 1977), 116. © Copyright 1977, 1989 by Billy Graham. Used by permission of Thomas Nelson, Inc. All rights reserved.

7. Marshall, *Mr. Jones*, 30–31. Used by permission.

8. Billy Graham, as quoted in *Quote Unquote*, ed. Lloyd Cory (Wheaton, Ill.: Victor Books, a division of SP Publications, 1977), 102.

9. Jeffrey L. Cotter, "Witness Upmanship," *Eternity*, March 1981, 22–23. Used by permission of Alliance of Confessing Evangelicals.

10. Jim Petersen, *Evangelism as a Lifestyle* (Colorado Springs: NavPress, 1980), 24–25.

11. Paul E. Little, *How to Give Away Your Faith* (Downers Grove, Ill.: InterVarsity, 1966), 37, 39. © 1988 by Marie Little. Used by permission of InterVarsity Press, P.O. Box 1400, Downers Grove, IL 60515. www.ivpress.com

12. Rebecca Manley Pippert, *Out of the Salt-Shaker and Into the World* (Downers Grove, Ill.: InterVarsity, 1979), 132–33. © 1979 by InterVarsity Christian Fellowship. Used by permission of InterVarsity Press, P.O. Box 1400, Downers Grove, IL 60515. www.ivpress.com

13. Billy Graham, as quoted in *Quote Unquote*, 102.

14. Earl D. Radmacher, "Salvation: A Necessary Work of God," in *Understanding Christian Theology*, ed. Charles R. Swindoll and Roy B. Zuck (Nashville: Thomas Nelson, 2003), 846.

15. Radmacher, "Salvation," 847–52.

We Are Here for You

We designed this volume of *LifeMaps* to help you on a
journey of lasting life-change. Along the way, you may
need further insight, encouragement, or simply prayer
with a fellow traveler. Insight for Living provides staff
pastors and women's counselors who are available for
free written correspondence or phone consultation.
These seminary-trained men and women have years of
pastoral experience and are well-qualified guides for
your spiritual journey.

Please feel welcome to contact our Pastoral Ministries
department by calling the Insight for Living Care Line:
(972) 473-5097, 8:00 a.m. through 5:00 p.m. Central
time. Or you may write to the following address:

Insight for Living
Pastoral Ministries Department
Post Office Box 269000
Plano, Texas 75026-9000

Ordering *Information*

If you would like to order additional *LifeMaps* or other
Insight for Living resources, please contact the office
that serves you.

Insight for Living
Post Office Box 269000
Plano, Texas 75026-9000
1-800-772-8888 toll-free
972-473-5136 international
www.insight.org

Insight for Living Australia
Post Office Box 1011
Bayswater, VIC 3153
AUSTRALIA
1 300 467 444 toll-free
www.insight.asn.au

Insight for Living Canada
Post Office Box 2510
Vancouver, BC V6B 3W7
1-800-663-7639 toll-free
www.insightforliving.ca

Insight for Living United Kingdom
Post Office Box 348
Leatherhead
KT22 2DS
UNITED KINGDOM
0800 915 93 64 toll-free
www.insightforliving.org.uk